OXWELL'S LIMERICAL ATLAS OF FLORIDA

Coupled with Select
Observations
on External Locales

Written by C. Mike Oxwell

Illustrated by Wilma Fine-Guerdoux

Printed in the United States of America. No part of this book may be used or reproduced in any manner whatsoever without written permission except in the case of brief quotations embedded in critical articles and reviews. For information, address Bar Addonizio Publishing, Burlington, Vermont, baraddonizio@gmail.com.

First Bar Addonizio paperback edition published in 2024

By C. Mike Oxwell
Illustrated by Wilma Fine-Guerdoux
Designed by Hannah Wood

ISBN: 979-8-218-42083-3

Subject:
HUM005000 HUMOR / Form / Limericks & Verse
HUM008000 HUMOR / Topic / Adult
HUM021000 HUMOR / Topic / Regional & Cultural

Library of Congress Cataloging-in-Publication data is available upon request.

CONTENTS

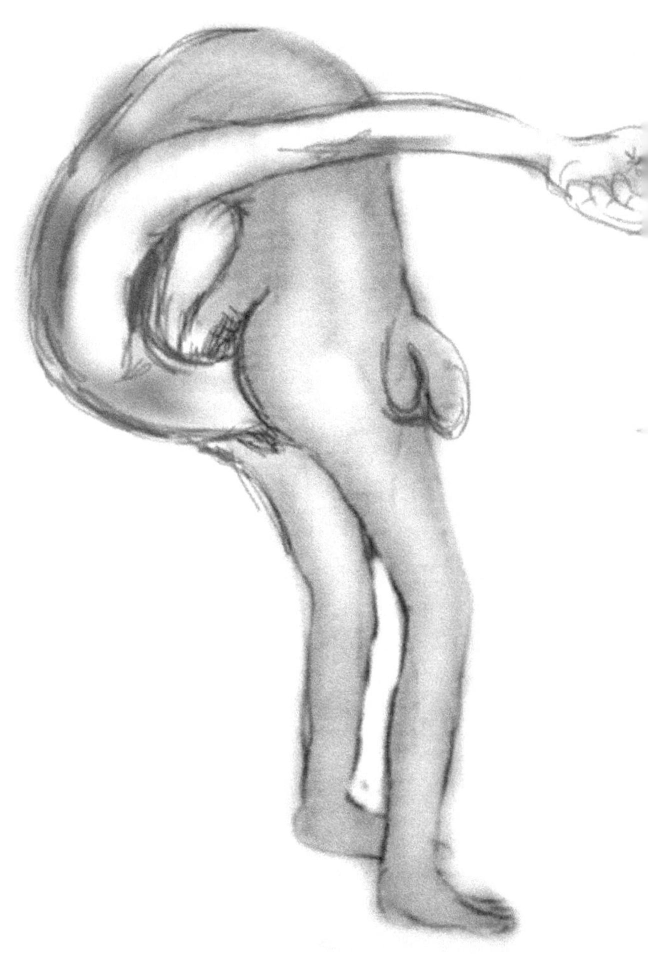

INTRODUCTION

We Are in Florida;

Florida Is in Us

So first: why Florida? What has Florida done to us, that we should make it the subject of a whole book of rude and mostly X-rated limericks? If we must defame a state, why not make it Georgia or Alabama, or someplace truly sketchy, as for instance Texas?[1]

But we write and draw what we know and love. Florida is our home. The two of us have lived here for over

---

[1] Birthplace of the author.

seventy combined years. Our work is here; our lives are here. By the flexible standards suited to a state full of transients, we consider ourselves natives.

As for the various Florida municipalities named in these limericks: it is our earnest desire to make every one of them as famous as Nantucket. On this score, the Florida Chamber of Commerce itself should endorse our aims. And we hope this work of ours will in some small way help demonstrate that not only do we Floridians have the best citrus and theme parks and beaches, the best sports teams and hotels and politicians: we also bid fair to have the best limerick characters. Whenever—as will sometimes happen—the course of literary events requires that a gentleman sodomize himself with a garden implement, we can count on there being a man in Egypt Lake equal to the task. This, too, is part of what makes Florida great.

Of course it should go without saying that no actual defamation is being attempted here. By their nature, limericks make no truth-claims. No one believes that the celebrated man from Nantucket ever really existed. And even if he had, his existence would in no way constitute an indictment of his hometown. The same principle holds for the various men, women, trans people, and animals who populate the following pages.

Rather than being statements of fact, limericks are a kind of language-game: a group of words that risibly satisfies certain unusual rules of arrangement. Included among those rules—along with specifics of meter and rhyme and subject-matter—is the appearance of a place-name at the end of the poem's opening line, where it determines the first of the two rhymes that recur throughout the piece. If, bowing to current theoretical fashion, we split the place-name into its two necessary halves, the signifier (the spoken and written forms of the name itself) and the signified (the geographical place to which the name refers), limericks generally concentrate on the former. Nantucket is an important place-name for limericks not because of the topography of the place to which it refers or because of that place's famed historical associations with whaling, but because of the rhyming possibilities the sound of the name creates. Allowing for necessary changes of context, the same holds true of all the proper nouns in the following pages. It may be granted that most limericks do aim to offend, in the broadest sense of the term. But they are not designed to convey offense to specific persons or places.

As to the more general tone of rudeness, this too has over time become one of the conventions of the limerick form. But it does not seem to have been so at first. The earliest recognizable collections of limericks to appear in print, in England in the 1820s, are closer in spirit to nursery rhymes than to any sort of obscene writing. Here is the anonymous *History of Sixteen Wonderful Old Women* (1820) with a typical bit of silliness:

> There was an old woman in Spain,
> To be civil went much 'gainst her grain;
> Yet she danced a fandango
> With General Fernando
> This whimsical woman of Spain[2].

And here, in the same vein and with the same first-line repetition, is Edward Lear (1861):

> There was an Old Man on a hill,
> Who seldom, if ever, stood still;
> He ran up and down,
> In his Grandmother's gown,
> Which adorned that Old Man on a hill.[3]

---

[2]*The History of Sixteen Wonderful Old Women, illustrated by as many engravings: exhibiting their Principal Eccentricities and Amusements* (London, 1820); rpt. Iona and Peter Opie, eds., *A Nursery Companion* (Oxford: Oxford UP, 1980), 69. Online facsimile at The Hockliffe Project, De Montfort University, Leicester, UK: http://www.sd-editions.com/hockliffeNew/items/0569I.html.
[3]Edward Lear, *The Complete Verse and Other Nonsense*, ed. Vivien Noakes (London; Penguin, 2002), 158.

Cross-dressing grandsons notwithstanding, one senses no indecency in these early limericks. The feeling is more droll and eccentric.

The indecency arrives soon, however. By 1870, for example, the anonymous *Cythera's Hymnal* offers the following elegant verses:

> There was a young lass of Blackheath
> Who frigged an old man with her teeth.
> She complained that he stunk
> Not so much from the spunk,
> But his arsehole was just underneath.[+]

Here already is the modern dirty limerick in its perfected form, with the old-fashioned repetition of the first-line rhyme word gone and with unabashed focus on both of the modern limerick's main subjects: sex and scatology. From here the road leads straight to more recent compositions like the ones in this collection.

[+]*Cythera's Hymnal, or Flakes from the Foreskin* ([Oxford], 1870), rpt. G. Legman, ed., *The Limerick: 1700 Examples, with Notes Variants and Index* (New York: Bell, 1964), 384. A secretly printed anthology of erotic material that includes the earliest surviving collection of dirty limericks, *Cythera's Hymnal* is for obvious reasons a rare book. It was apparently assembled by the journalist George Augustus Sala, with contributions from a number of other figures active in the world of Victorian erotica (Peter Mendes, *Clandestine Erotic Fiction in English 1800-1902: A Bibliographical Study* [Aldershot: Scolar P, 1993], 234).

It is a nice question just how and why the limerick turned dirty in this way. But in any case, the obscenity marks not so much an innovation as a reversion: a turn back to subject-matter far older than any kind of children's literature. Here, for instance, is one of Martial's obscene epigrams from the 1st century AD:

> Quod pectus, quod crura tibi, quod bracchia vellis,
>> quod cincta est brevibus mentula tonsa pilis,
>> hoc praestas, Labiene, tuae (quis nescit ?) amicae.
>> cui praestas, culum quod, Labiene, pilas?[5]

> You shave your arms, legs, chest, and dick, they say,
>> Because your girlfriend likes them best that way.
>> But Labienus, dare I ask for whom
>> You shave your stinky brown-eyed crack of doom?

Let us admit straightaway that our translation cheapens the original. Where Martial uses the one word "culum," we introduce a six-word mixed metaphor drawn straight from the school playground. The result is a sillier, more childish, more scatological poem than Martial's. But even so, and despite 1800 years age difference and the language barrier, Martial's epigram has more in common with *Cythera's Hymnal,*

---

[5]M. Val. Martialis, *Epigrammata*, ed. W. M. Lindsay (Oxford: Oxford UP, 1922), II.62.

on the level of substance, than either has in common with the limericks of Lear.

What happens, we think, is that the limerick first emerges as a children's form, but proves so rich in comic possibilities that older, more traditional kinds of humor lay claim to it after its initial appearance and turn it after the fact into an adults-only genre. It is a case of obscene subject-matter searching out its ideal formal expression. And despite its lack of critical esteem, the limerick remains to this day the go-to metrical form for anyone writing obscene epigrams in English.

This is so, we believe, for mostly formal reasons. From the standpoint of the comedian, the best thing about the limerick is its extreme obliquity. The requirements of rhyme and meter force one sideways, into intricate detours, in the process of saying the simplest thing. We once read somewhere that in former days, the Chinese civil service entrance exam required applicants to rewrite a 500-word essay at twice that length, without introducing any new information. Despite their compression, limericks do something similar: they force the author to subordinate sense to style in ways so improbable as to be inherently amusing. So it seems natural that the earliest limericks should have been nonsense verse. (In fact, "nonsense" is the word

12

Lear used for his limericks, the word "limerick" itself not yet being associated with the verse form.) And when the form finally does attach to conventional subject-matter, it seems right that the matter in question should be as silly and vulgar as possible. In the nonsensical upside-down world of the limerick, it's only right that the genitals should rule the head.

In any case, limericks have always valued style over substance. That, arguably, is why the earliest practitioners of the form include a series of eccentric and/or rebellious figures with an affinity for Pre-Raphaelitism and aestheticism: not just Lear but also A. C. Swinburne, D. G. Rossetti, and Aubrey Beardsley.[6] In their way, these men

---

[6]Like much other Victorian erotica, Swinburne's limericks have mostly disappeared. For what is known of them, see Bob Turvey, "The Limericks of Algernon Swinburne," *Journal of Pre-Raphaelite Studies* 20 (Fall, 2011), 63-71. The main surviving body of Rossetti's limericks was collected by the poet's brother in *The Works of Dante Gabriel Rossetti*, ed. William M. Rossetti (London: Ellis, 1911), 273-275. The *OED* cites a passage from Beardsley's letters as the earliest recorded usage of the noun "limerick" in reference to the poetic form (John Simpson and E. S. P. Weiner, eds., *The Oxford English Dictionary*, 20 vols. [Oxford: Clarendon, 1989], "Limerick" sb. 1.). The letter, dating to early May of 1896 and addressed to the publisher and erotomane Leonard Smithers, refers to the artist's struggle with tuberculosis: "I have tried to amuse myself by writing limericks on my troubles but have got no further than[:] There once was a young invalid/ Whose lung would do nothing but bleed" (*The Letters of Aubrey Beardsley*, ed. Henry Maas, J. L. Duncan, and W. G. Good [Cranbury, NJ: Fairleigh Dickinson UP, 1970], 128).

all shared a loose commitment to the notion of art for art's sake. They all, to one degree or another, opposed the idea that art should be subservient to something else—society, truth, utility, morality—and they all looked to the work of art to provide its own justification. In both its technical precision and its contempt for conventional manners, the dirty limerick may be best understood as a minor expression of *fin de siècle* literary decadence.

If anything, this applies doubly to the beheaded limericks that make up about a quarter of this collection. Like other specialized sorts of limerick, the beheaded limerick ratchets up the form's difficulty by introducing a new set of technical requirements in addition to the customary ones. In the beheaded limerick's case, the new conditions involve a series of word scrambles, as one word in each line is split in half and the order of the two halves reversed, with the originally former (now latter) half providing the rhyme for each line. The resulting poetry sacrifices acoustic effect so as to become a mainly literary construct. It is hard to understand via recitation, and the splitting of words creates novel associations of meaning best recognized on the page. Here, for instance, an oft-quoted verse by Arthur Shaw teases out the lack (and addle) in Cadillac:

> A certain young pate who was addle
> Rode a horse he alleged to be saddle,

> But his gust which was dis
> For his haps which were mis
> Sent him back to his lac which was Cadil.[7]

An icon of success translates before our eyes into an emblem of incompetent privilege, with the very syllables of the icon's name being deployed against its iconicity. But for our purposes, the advantage of the beheaded limerick remains mainly technical: it gives us new resources with which to celebrate a number of fine Florida municipalities not easily assimilated to the regular limerick. (We dare you to write a regular limerick about Wewahitchka.)

So what moves us to add our own offerings to this distinguished literary tradition? How do we contribute to the evolution of the limerick form?

To begin with, this book represents the first time a limericist has ever undertaken a systematic town-by-town survey of any particular nation, state, or province. To be fair, the anonymous *A Peep at the Geography of Europe* did something similar around 1824, but its fifteen limericks ranged loosely and un-methodically across a whole continent. By contrast, our limericks move in detail across the length and breadth of Florida, covering almost all of its largest

---

[7] *The Penguin Book of Limericks*, ed. E. O. Parrott (London: Penguin, 1984), 256.

cities and many minor ones as well, before finally expanding to an additional group of verses on more far-flung places. In this way our venture crosses literary genres, invoking the grand tradition of travel-writing that extends from Herodotus to Lonely Planet and includes, in the process, such Florida classics as William Bartram's *Travels* and Gloria Jahoda's *The Other Florida*. While we dare not insert ourselves into such august company, we do hope to supply an alternative travelogue, as it were, for Florida: a picture of the state as it might exist in another dimension, on a different, sillier and hornier version of our planet.

This book is also organized unlike any other collection of limericks. The poems themselves appear in six regional categories drawn from the travel literature that has partly inspired us: the Panhandle; Jacksonville and the Space Coast; Orlando and Central Florida ; Tampa and the Gulf Coast; South Florida and the Keys; and finally, the additional poems relating to external places. (Within each category we have proceeded more freely.) These divisions enable readers to conduct an area-specific study of the state's sexual practices and to develop, in the process, a deepening respect for the diversity of Floridian local culture. In addition, we then provide two indexes for further specialized consultation: one regular alphabetical index organized according to city, and also a subject index organized according to the different versions of perversion that appear in our pages. Together, these reference tools allow unique kinds of access to the poems here presented.

Our illustrations deserve mention as well, although in their case we make no claim to novelty. Instead, the pictures revive a well-established but more recently neglected practice. The first-generation limerick books of the 1820s were all illustrated. The artist for two of them—*The Anecdotes and Adventures of Fifteen Gentlemen* (1821) and the *Anecdotes and Adventures of Fifteen Young Ladies* (c. 1822)—appears to have been Isaac Robert Cruikshank, elder brother to the caricaturist George. Edward Lear, an illustrator before he became a poet, supplied drawings for both his collections of limericks. And Lear's work offers precedent for the more recent illustrated limericks of Edward Gorey.[8] But other collections of the twentieth century—for instance Gershon Legman's massive anthology *The Limerick* and the two collections co-authored by Isaac Asimov and John Ciardi[9]—neglect this connection between the sister

[8] Edward Gorey, *The Listing Attic* (Boston: Little, Brown and Company, 1954).

[9] Isaac Asimov and John Ciardi, *Limericks: Too Gross and A Grossery of Limericks* (New York: W. W. Norton, 1978 and 1981). Legman's collection is cited above, n. 4.

[10] Anthony Madrid, "Anthony Madrid's Limericks. Illustrated by Mark Fletcher," Body (December 23, 2013), http://bodyliterature/anthony-madrid-illustrated-limericks/.

arts. More recently still, Anthony Madrid and Mark Fletcher have revived the pairing of limericks with illustrations, and we hope to continue this worthy trend here.

Finally, we might describe the experience of composing and illustrating these poems as an agreeable kind of insanity. One does not impose one's will on the words; if anything, the reverse is true, and in the happiest cases the words press the author into meaning.

And somehow or other, we are convinced that Florida has helped. Perhaps it has something to do with the state's shape on a map, or the fact that Florida is a peninsula, a word just four letters long of "penis." Then again, perhaps it has to do with the design of the state capitol building, built in the late 1970s under Governor Reuben Askew and casually known to locals as Reuben's Erection. But for whatever reason, our home state has lent us rich resources and much inspiration in our undertaking. We acknowledge the debt with gratitude and affection.

LIMERICKS

Part One:

The Panhandle

1 * Navarre

There was a young man from Navarre
Whose appetite proved most bizarre.
He'd only eat quim
On days starting with M
During months with names ending in R.

---

2 * Pensacola

A gramps from sacola that's Pen
Lost track of his tures that were den
In the muu that was muu
Of a zy that was floo
While he tongued her italia that's gen.

3 ∗ Bonifay

Two gastronomes from Bonifay
Got booked for indecent display
When thrusting their cocks
In the bagels and lox
At a Bob's Big Boy breakfast buffet.

————

4 ∗ Wewahitchka

A guy from wahitchka that's We
Had a substandard nis that was pe,
All torted that's con
And dersized that was un
And deficient in men that is se.

5 * Lynn Haven

A handsome young man from Lynn Haven
Considered himself a poon maven,
Skilled with blonde or brunette,
Black or white, dry or wet,
Hairy, sculpted, trimmed, tattooed, or shaven.

———

6 * Chattahoochee

A demoiselle from Chattahoochee
Would only wear fashion by Gucci—
Hat, handbag, or shoes,
Satin, silk, or charmeuse,
On her head or her feet or her coochie.

7 * Carrabelle

There was a young lady from Carrabelle
Much noted in fable and parable
For dresses so slight
And disturbingly tight
That the mayor pronounced them unwearable.

8 * Tallahassee

Our governor Ron and his spouse
Together might make a whole louse.
They claimed to be tough
And to have the right stuff,
But then got their ass kicked by a mouse.

9 * Monticello

A pretty girl from Monticello
Once grew up inside a bordello.
She learned to suck dick
For ten dollars a trick
And to wrestle all comers in jello.

10 * Perry

There was a young lady from Perry
Who lost her proverbial cherry
One fine Christmas Eve
To a Santa named Steve,
Seven elves, and a sugarplum fairy.

11 * Cedar Key

A redneck from near Cedar Key
Once went on a sexual spree.
He buggered two beavers,
Three golden retrievers,
And one underage manatee.

12 * Lake City

There was a young man from Lake City
Who thought himself terribly pretty,
For his beard looked like bush
And his forehead like tush
And his face like Glen Close's left titty.

13 ✶ Bronson

A clever young fellow from Bronson
Once had an exceptional Johnson.
Just south of the head
Lay a birthmark in red
That was shaped like the state of Wisconsin

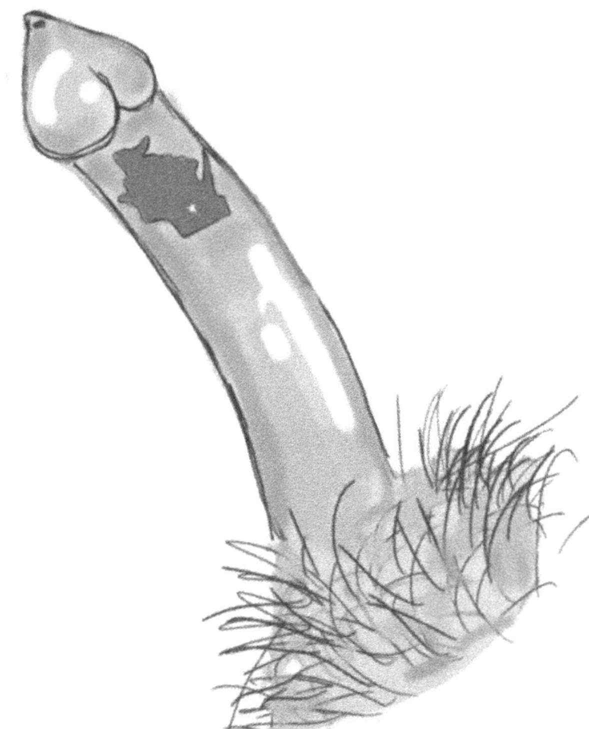

Part Two

Jacksonville & the Space Coast

1 * Archer

I know a young fellow from Archer
Whose scrotum could hardly be larger.
When air travel calls,
He positions his balls
In the overhead bin for departure.

2 * High Springs

A madam from Springs known as High
Was known to be assed that is bi
Toward the finements called re
In the sign known as de
Of her favorite brator that's vi.

3 ★ Brooker

A young vice detective from Brooker
Fell madly in love with a hooker.
He was in such a lather
He didn't know whether
To marry her, pay her, or book her.

4 * Palatka

A gourmet from latka that's Pa
Once tasted a lut that was ba,
Liked rian that's du,
Enjoyed gu that was fu,
But preferred his own ca that was ca.

5 * Jacksonville

A teacher from sonville that's Jack
Used to write on the board known as black
While her dents that were stu
All grew mescent that's tu
From inspecting her side that was back.

6 ∗ Beverly Beach

A lawyer from Beverly Beach
Filed suit for material breach
When an unlucky stripper
Got caught in his zipper
While giving his privates a reach.

7 ∗ DeLand

There was a young girl from DeLand
Who used to put out on demand.
She sucked all the cream
From the basketball team
And finished the mascot by hand.

8 * DeBary

A Liberty Mom from DeBary
Once liked the odd tumbler of sherry.
A couple of those
And she'd discard her clothes
And sell off her ass cash-and-carry.

9 * Deltona

A teenie from tona called Del
Engaged in the latio that's fel
Till the stick known as joy
On her friend known as boy
Filled her mouth with atine we call gel.

10 ⋆ Rockledge

A fellow from ledge known as Rock
Took part in a fight known as cock,
But a pon that was ca
Pecked his dolph that was A
Till it hid in his strap that was jock.

11 ⋆ Cocoa

A pretty young lady from Cocoa
Once drove all the neighbor boys loco,
Inhaling their stones
And then blowing their bones
With the force of a raging scirocco.

Part Three:

Orlando &
Central
Florida

1 * Bushnell

A lovely young lass from Bushnell
Fellated a man in a well.
The well was artesian
And warmed their cohesion,
Thus helping his Johnson to swell.

2 * Astatula

A prostitute from Astatula
Once made herself buckets of moolah
By shaking her ass
In a skirt made of grass,
Giving blowjobs, and dancing the hula.

3 * Altamonte Springs

A housewife from Altamonte Springs
Insists upon sex with no strings,
But likes ropes and chains,
Has a nice set of canes,
And owns one of those flexible swings.

4 * Dundee

A lady from dee that is Dun
Was concerned for her nikin that's cun,
Since a charge we call dis
Proved its tress that was mis
Had contracted a gus that was fun.

5 ⋆ Winter Park

A gentleman from Winter Park
Screwed his sister one night for a lark,
And thereof ensued
A vociferous brood:
Three whinny, one talks, and two bark.

6 ⋆ Windermere

A lady from mere that was Winder
Once suffered a bender that's fender.
A truck that was Mack
Banged her side that was back
Right in front of a garten that's kinder.

7 * Orlando

A pretty young lad from Orlando
Once caused an amusement-park scandal,
Encouraging Mickey
To get his butt sticky
While bringing off Donald by hand-o.

8 * Celebration

A gentleman from Celebration
Became a true Disney sensation:
He bayed at the moon
To a Britney Spears tune
While fucking his neighbor's Dalmatian.

9 * Lake Hart

An elderly man from Lake Hart
Once let a deplorable fart.
The smell of his feces
Endangered two species
And gassed out the local Walmart.

10 * Kissimmee

There was a young lady named Kimmie
Who hailed from beshitten Kissimmee.
She proved so encouraging
To each little urging
That folks called her Kimmie the Gimme.

———

11 * Lake Wales

A pretty young lass from Lake Wales
Abandoned conventional males
Because she preferred
A more high-minded herd:
Now her daughters and sons all have tails.

12 * Lakeland

A fellow from land that is Lake
Was an infamous hell known as rake:
He even chowed down
On an ie that was brown
In the midst of a sale that was bake.

13 * Fort Meade

There was a young man from Fort Meade
Who'd never been taught how to breed.
So he did it all wrong
By installing his dong
In a cavity not meant for seed.

Part Four:

Tampa & the Gulf Coast

1 * Zephyrhills

A lady from hills that were Zephyr
Was famed for her ance that's persever.
In suit that was pur
Of the burger that's fur
She was said to be lasting that's ever.

2 * Egypt Lake

A gentleman from Egypt Lake
Had intercourse once with a rake.
He said it was passionate
However you fashion it—
But oh how his asshole did ache!

3 * Largo

A sickly old fellow from Largo
Had bowels overflowing with cargo,
Yet although he'd strain,
It was all done in vain,
For his butt had imposed an embargo.

4 * Redington Shores

The ladies from Redington Shores
Are famous for all being whores.
They're quick to chomp choad
And to swallow the load,
And they're lightning at dropping their drawers.

5 * Riverview

A gentleman from Riverview
Was officially too blind to screw.
He sought out a whorehouse
But turned at a storehouse
And wound up instead at the zoo.

6 ⋆ Tampa

A lovely young lady from Tampa
Was famous for being a tramp-a.
She knew all her friends
In the Biblical sense
And fellated her BFF's grampa.

7 ⋆ Palmetto

A tenor from metto that's Pal
Used to sing in a setto that's fal
When his bund that was cummer
And wear that were unner
Constricted his sack that was ball.

8 ✳ Sarasota

A sweetheart from sota that's Sara
Spent time in a van known as cara,
Where the nads that were go
Of some mads that were no
Got a taste of her schino that's mara.

---

9 ✳ Port Charlotte

The ladies who live in Port Charlotte
Are markedly different from our lot.
They can all suck the chrome
Off a Cadillac Brougham
And shag like a Hollywood[11] harlot.

---

[11] See 5.16.

10 * Cape Coral

There was a young man from Cape Coral
Whose character proved most immoral.
In sexual sessions
He liked all transgressions,
The vaginal, anal, and oral.

11 * Fort Myers

A pretty young lass from Fort Myers
Was mad about cables and wires.
She shoved a receiver
So deep in her beaver
They had to extract it with pliers.

12 ∗ Sanibel

A sweetie from bel known as Sani
Departed for da we call Cana
When her hubby that's ex
Aired a tape that's called sex
Of her fucking a na we call bana.

12 ∗ Sanibel

Part Five:

South Florida & the Keys

1 * Fort Pierce

There was a young lass from Fort Pierce
With cunts where most people have ears.
She got trichomonas,
Which came with a bonus:
A vaginal case of Ménière's.

2 * Pahokee

A pretty young gal from Pahokee
Got fucked once by Gumby and Pokey.
As Gumby let loose
With a stream of green juice,
Pokey entered her Okeefenokee.

3 * Belle Glade

A general's wife from Belle Glade
Was obsessive about getting laid.
While her husband would do
Regimental review
She could screw an entire brigade.

4 * Naples

A Nazi from Naples named Rick
Grew wealthy defrauding the sick,
Then got off Scott-free
With a no-contest plea,
Since he knew the right assholes to lick.

5 * Glen Ridge

An alkie from Ridge that is Glen
Embarked on a der known as ben
Till his bations called li
Caused arrhea that's di
To gush out of his trails known as en.

6 * Boca Raton

A surfer from Boca Raton
Once tried to make love to a prawn,
But sadly his shrimp
Remained listless and limp
And could not be persuaded to spawn.

7 ∗ Palm Beach

An orange-hued turd from Palm Beach
Offers wisdom no one can impeach,
Sharing nuclear codes
In his varied abodes,
Grabbing pussy, and shooting up bleach.

8 ∗ Briny Breezes

The debutantes of Briny Breezes
Are famous for all being teases,
Unless you've got dough—
Then they act like a ho
And infect you with horrid diseases.

9 * Coconut Creek

A fellow from Coconut Creek
Had a dick that was painfully weak.
It shrank from temptation
And firm provocation,
And dribbled while taking a leak.

10 ✳ Sunrise

A fellow from rise that's called Sun
Engaged in nilingus called cun
With a ny that was gran
With a ny that was cran
With an odor like dungus that's mun.

11 ✳ Plantation

A lady from tation called Plan
Fell in love with a dog we call ban
Till the vor that was fer
Of her version that's per
Made her marry a drill that was man.

12 ⭑ Hollywood[12]

The ladies of wood known as Holly
Enjoy having ances called dalli
With each ron that's mo
And each do known as do
Who's endowed with a whacker that's tally.

13 ⭑ Davie

I knew a beach bunny from Davie,
With hair that was golden and wavy,
Who acted obscene
With the merchant marine
And fucked half the Bahamian navy.

---

[12] See 4.11

14 ⋆ Fort Lauderdale

A man from Fort dale known as Lauder,
When hot, lost all ation that's moder,
And found lief that's re
From his ver that was fe
Through a passion for sports that are water.

---

15 ⋆ Miramar

A glutton from mar that is Mira
Once gorged on misu that is tira,
Till the product that's by
Of his gestion that's di
Formed a sizeable mid that was pyra.

16 * Aventura

A gentleman from Aventura
Once suffered from pain of the pleura,
But sniffing of quim
Got his lungs fit and trim,
So he learned how to lick with bravura.

17 * Hialeah

A Cuban man from Hialeah
Contracted severe gonorrhea
By banging his maid
With such force that he sprayed
His *crema* into her *tortilla.*

18 ∗ Miami

A clever young man from Miami
Once tried to seduce a gourami,
But sadly his dick
Was afflicted with ick
And her lips were appallingly clammy.

19 ∗ Key Biscayne

A gentleman from Key Biscayne
Found such extreme pleasure in pain,
One couldn't determine
What more pleased the vermin:
To torture him or to refrain.

20 * Key West

A lady I knew from Key West
Was only a lady in jest,
For under her clothes
She was packing a hose,
And her boob job was none of the best.

Part 6:

External Locales

1 ✻ Vancouver

I know a young lass from Vancouver
Who sucks with the force of a Hoover.
When once she connects
With an organ of sex,
A crowbar's required to remove her.

2 ✻ Kaiser, MO

There was a young lady from Kaiser
Who had an affair with a ricer.
She jammed a potater
Up into her crater
And mashed it and came like a geyser.

3 ⋆ Rueter, MO

There was a young lady from Rueter
Who had an adjustable cooter.
A twist of her tit
Would adapt her to fit
Any Tom, Dick, or Harry who screwed her.

4 ⋆ Mingus, TX

I know a young Texan from Mingus
Who has a diminutive dingus,
Because of which foible
He's only employable
For purposes of cunnilingus.

5 ✶ North Carolina

A cutie from North Carolina
Possessed an expansive vagina.
Aroused and extended,
The dicks she befriended
Would reach from Peru clear to China.

———

6 ✶ Moultrie, GA

There was a young lady from Moultrie
Who felt very close to her poultry.
She clucked and she nested
Till finally arrested
For lewd gallinaceous adultery.

7 * Durham

An elderly fellow from Durham
Could not keep his longfellow firm.
Viagra, Cialis,
Two tongues on his phallus:
No, nothing was able to cure him.

8 * Alblasserdam

A lady from Alblasserdam
Was a true connoisseur of the clam,
Whether steamed, raw, or fried,
Or best, nestled inside
Of a succulent wallet of ham.

9 * Spain

There was a young fellow from Spain
Whose butt got confused with his brain.
He talked diarrhea
Sans sense or idea
Till squatting and starting to strain.

But soon as the straining had started,
His eloquence dashed the fainthearted,
For the breath of his words
Held an odor of turds.
When he spoke, we all thought that he'd farted.

10 * Karachi

Two good Muslim lads from Karachi
Grilled sausages on an hibachi.
They couldn't eat pig,
But their wieners were big,
And delicious with mirin and dashi.

11 ✳ Rangoon

There was a young man from Rangoon
Who never wore condoms for poon,
For from illness venereal
And such like material
The poon in Rangoon was immune.

But if you think the poon in Rangoon
Is immune, then watch out for your prune,
For you may as securely
And equally purely
Go swim in a public spittoon.

12 ✱ Fuzhou

A zoo scientist from Fuzhou
Fell madly in love with a cow.
She was named Genevieve
And on visiting leave
From the Universidad de Bilbao.

———

13 ✱ Chengdu

A lovely young girl from Chengdu
Once studied the art of kung fu.
She could maim with her fist
Or a flick of her wrist,
And she had a near-lethal bazoo.

14 ✱ Penang

A Taoist who lived in Penang
Invented a new way to bang.
He stretched out his willy
And bent it until he
Inserted his yin in his yang.

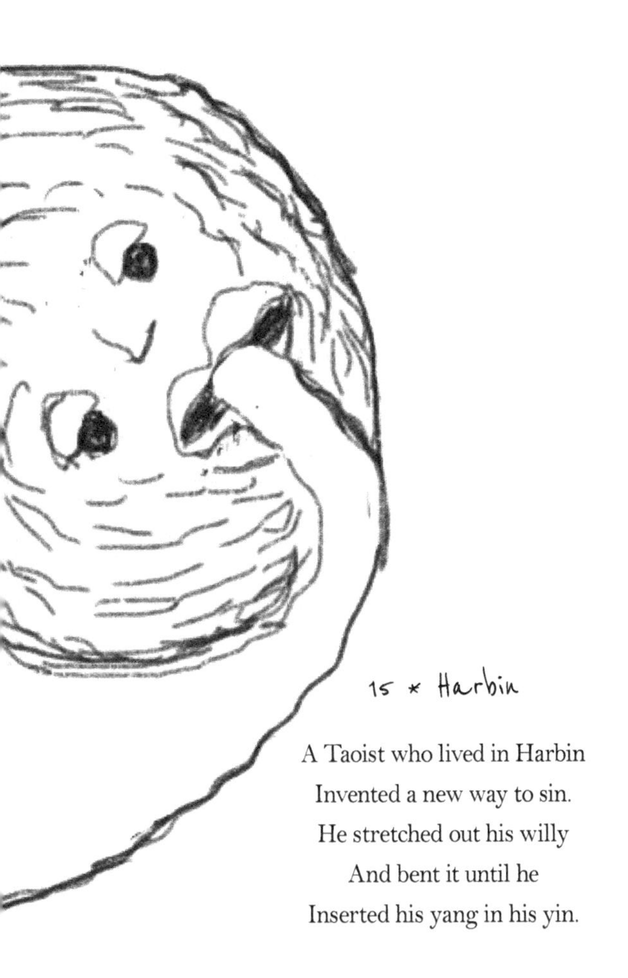

15 * Harbin

A Taoist who lived in Harbin
Invented a new way to sin.
He stretched out his willy
And bent it until he
Inserted his yang in his yin.

ALPHABETICAL INDEX

Moultrie, GA: 6.6
Naples: 5.4
Navarre: 1.1
North Carolina: 6.5
Orlando: 3.7
Pahokee: 5.2
Palatka: 2.4
Palm Beach: 5.7
Palmetto: 4.7
Penang: 6.14
Pensacola: 1.2
Perry: 1.10
Plantation: 5.11
Port Charlotte: 4.9
Rangoon: 6.11
Redington Shores: 4.4
Riverview: 4.5
Rockledge: 2.10
Rueter, MO: 6.3
Sanibel: 4.12
Sarasota: 4.8
Spain: 6.9
Sunrise: 5.10
Tallahassee: 1.8
Tampa: 4.6
Vancouver: 6.1
Wewahitchka: 1.4
Windermere: 3.6
Winter Park: 3.5
Zephyrhills: 4.1

SUBJECT INDEX

2.6 (Beverly Beach); 2.8 (DeBarry); 3.2 (Astatula); 5.8 (Briny Breezes)

Questionable Characters: 1.5 (Lynn Haven); 1.8 (Tallahassee); 1.10 (Perry); 2.3 (Brooker); 2.8 (DeBarry); 3.10 (Kissimmee); 3.13 (Fort Meade); 4.1 (Zephyrhills); 4.6 (Tampa); 4.8 (Sarasota); 4.9 (Port Charlotte); 4.10 (Cape Coral); 5.2 (Pahokee); 5.3 (Belle Glade); 5.7 (Palm Beach); 5.12 (Hollywood); 5.19 (Key Biscayne); 5.20 (Key West); 6.11 (Rangoon); 6.14 (Penang); 6.15 (Harbin)

Sports Fans: 2.7 (Deland); 5.6 (Boca Raton); 5.14 (Fort Lauderdale); 6.13 (Chengdu)

Things You Can Do with Fruit: 4.12 (Sanibel)

Wardrobe Malfunctions: 1.6 (Chattahoochee); 1.7 (Carabelle); 4.7 (Palmetto)

www.ingramcontent.com/pod-product-compliance
Lightning Source LLC
Chambersburg PA
CBHW041210150726
48006CB00016B/2194